FRONTLINE
FAMILIES

THE AMERICAN REVOLUTION

Frontline Soldiers and Their Families

Sara Howell

Gareth Stevens
PUBLISHING

Please visit our website, **www.garethstevens.com**. For a free color catalog of all our
high-quality books, call toll free 1-800-542-2595 or fax 1-877-542-2596.

Library of Congress Cataloging-in-Publication Data
Howell, Sara.
The American Revolution: frontline soldiers and their families / by Sara Howell.
p. cm. — (Frontline families)
Includes index.
ISBN 978-1-4824-3053-0 (pbk.)
ISBN 978-1-4824-3056-1 (6 pack)
ISBN 978-1-4824-3054-7 (library binding)
1. United States — History — Revolution, 1775-1783 — Juvenile literature.
2. United States — History — Revolution, 1775 - 1783 — Social aspects — Juvenile literature.
I. Howell, Sara. II. Title.
E208.H69 2016
973.3—d23

First Edition

Published in 2016 by
Gareth Stevens Publishing
111 East 14th Street, Suite 349
New York, NY 10003

© 2016 Gareth Stevens Publishing

Produced by Calcium
Editors for Calcium: Sarah Eason and Rachel Warren Chadd
Designers: Paul Myerscough and Jessica Moon
Picture researcher: Susannah Jayes

Picture credits: Cover: Wikipedia Commons: A. M. Willard/Abbot Hall MA; Inside: Shutterstock:
AISA/Everett 21, American Spirit 5tl, 5tr, 30, 35, Nicku 16–17, Vladimir Korostyshevskiy 44,
Ken Schulze 29br; Wikimedia Commons: 7r, 12, 15br, 25l, 25tr, 32, 33, 37, A. M. Willard/
Abbot Hall MA 34, AgnosticPreachersKid 45tl, Domenick D'Andrea 11, Center for Jewish
History 42, Google Cultural Institute 8, Harper's Magazine 39tr, Humanitiesweb.org 15tl, The
Indian Reporter 41tl, Library of Congress 4, 9, 13, 17tr, 20, 26, 29tr, Lilly Library, University of
Indiana 23br, Massachusetts Historical Society 28, Metropolitan Museum 25bl, Mitchell Map
Company 6, Mwanner 31l, Museum of Fine Arts, Boston 18br, 27, National Archives and Records
Administration 40, 43br, New York Public Library Digital Collection 18tr, Project Gutenberg 31tr,
Ben Schumin 45tr, David Shankbone 43tl, US Capitol 23t, 38, U.S. Diplomacy Center 39l, White
House Historical Association 7tl.

Printed in the United States of America

CPSIA compliance information: Batch #CS15GS: For further information contact Gareth Stevens, New York, New York at 1-800-542-2595.

CONTENTS

CHAPTER 1

LIFE IN THE COLONIES

A revolution is a complete change in a country's government. In the course of history, some revolutions have been peaceful. Many, though, have been fought as bloody wars. The revolution that shaped the United States was one such war. For the war's duration and beyond, it would affect the lives of every man, woman, and child who lived through it, as well as generations to come.

Ruled from Afar

Before the American Revolution, the country that we know as the United States did not exist. Instead, there were 13 loosely connected British colonies along the Atlantic coast of North America. A colony is an area occupied and controlled by another, often distant, country—some of whose people settle there. From 1760, the British colonies of North America were ruled by King George III of Great Britain, a country across the Atlantic Ocean nearly 4,000 miles (6,500 km) away.

Legend has it that war widow Betsy Ross created the first American flag in 1776, but many now dispute this story.

This statue commemorates minutemen—Revolutionary War soldiers, ready to fight at a moment's notice.

During the war, British soldiers were often called redcoats because of their red uniforms.

Divided Loyalties

Over time, tensions grew between the colonists—mostly British people who had settled here—and the British government, especially over issues of taxes and money. Many colonists believed that they were being treated unfairly. They decided that their only choice was to declare themselves a new, independent country, free to make its own rules. Others, however, still considered themselves British citizens and did not want to go to war with their home country. Many neighbors were divided. There were even divided loyalties within families. Everyone in the colonies endured hardships and loss on the road to independence.

Revolutionary Legacy

The American Revolution was neither the longest nor the bloodiest war in US history, but it is one of the most important. It created the documents that designed the US government and shaped the country that America is today. In that sense, Americans still live with its effects.

FOUNDING OF THE COLONIES

When Christopher Columbus arrived in the New World in 1492, there was no way of knowing how the continent of North America would change over the next few hundred years. Different European countries, including Spain, Portugal, and France, founded colonies in the new land. However, it was England, which together with Wales and Scotland would later become Great Britain, that ultimately had the most success in colonizing what is now the East Coast of the United States.

Arrival of Settlers

The first permanent English settlement in North America was Jamestown, founded in the Colony of Virginia in 1607. A few years later, in 1620, the settlers we know as the Pilgrims arrived on the *Mayflower*. They created the Plymouth Colony, in Massachusetts.

Primary Source: What Does It Tell Us?

This map shows the 13 colonies at the time of the American Revolution. You might notice that all of the colonies are located near the Atlantic coast or a major river. What benefits would this offer families settling in the New World?

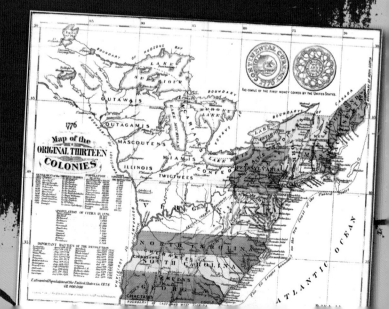

William Penn was the founder of Pennsylvania, which was a proprietary colony.

Types of Colonies

At the time before the American Revolution, the British had three types of colonies in North America—royal colonies, proprietary colonies, and charter colonies. A royal, or crown, colony was controlled by a governor who was chosen by the king. Just before the revolution, most of the 13 colonies were royal colonies. Proprietary colonies were areas of land given by the king to a person or family—usually to reward loyalty or service. The person, or proprietor, was responsible for governing the colony, but still answered to the king. Pennsylvania, Maryland, and Delaware were proprietary colonies.

In the third type of colony, the charter colony, the king granted a charter to the governing body of the colony. The charter was an official document setting out the rules by which the colony would be run. Connecticut and Rhode Island were both charter colonies. At any time, the king could revoke, or take away, the charter and turn the colony into a royal colony. The Massachusetts Bay Colony, for example, had its charter revoked in 1684.

A DELICATE RELATIONSHIP

The relationship between Great Britain and its North American colonies was an important and delicate one. Britain saw the colonies primarily as a way to raise money. Early settlers often went to the New World to make their fortunes. As time went on, though, many colonists began to see a chance to gain much more than money.

Fortune and Freedom

The colonies were important to Great Britain because they were rich in natural resources, such as lumber (forest wood) and furs. The early colonists—mainly men—came to North America thinking more about business ventures than raising families. They were tough but often not prepared for the harsh conditions. Many died from starvation and malnutrition. Other colonists, such as the Pilgrims, came to the New World looking for religious freedom. Many wanted to separate from the Church of England and form their own religious groups. To do so, they believed they would need to take some political control of their colonies.

George III reigned as the king of Great Britain from 1760 until his death in 1820.

Primary Source: What Does It Tell Us?

This political cartoon was designed by Benjamin Franklin in 1754 during the French and Indian War. The segments of the snake represent the colonies. The cartoon was meant to encourage unity among the colonies and convince them to join together with Great Britain against the French and Native Americans. The cartoon would later be used during the American Revolution to encourage the colonies to join forces against the British. How important do you think the notion of unity was in shaping the ideas of the American Revolution?

Family Life

The Pilgrims founded Plymouth Colony, in what is today Massachusetts. Conditions were harsh, but the settlers worked together to create one of the earliest successful British colonies in North America. Families usually included 5 to 6 children, though about 12 percent of children died before they turned a year old.

Surviving and Thriving

Over time, settlers learned to grow food and benefit from North America's resources. Though life was difficult, communities began to thrive and expand. Tobacco became an important crop, especially in the southern colonies. Colonists began bringing Africans to North America to work as slaves on their plantations. As colonies grew, their relationship with Britain and their forms of government became even more important issues.

A TIMELINE OF THE AMERICAN REVOLUTION

Officially, the American Revolution lasted a little less than eight years. However, the causes leading up to the war, as well as its effects, spanned decades. Here are a few of the important dates and events.

1754

May 28: The French and Indian War begins in North America with the Battle of Jumonville Glen. Though Great Britain would win, it emerged from the conflict deep in debt.

1763

October 7: George III issues a proclamation, designed to protect Native American land, which forbids the colonists from settling further west than the Appalachian Mountains.

1764

April 5: The Sugar Act is passed by the British Parliament, enforcing taxes on imported sugar and increasing taxes on coffee and wine.

1765

March 22: The British Parliament passes the Stamp Act–a direct tax on colonists, many of whom become concerned about "taxation without representation." It is repealed the next year.

1770

March 5: Five colonists are shot and killed by British soldiers in the Boston Massacre.

1773

December 16: A mob of colonists dump hundreds of crates of British tea into Boston Harbor in what will become known as the Boston Tea Party.

1774

September 5: Delegates to the First Continental Congress meet in Philadelphia.

1775

April 18: Paul Revere rides to alert colonial forces to the advance of British troops.

April 19: The battles of Lexington and Concord are fought.

May 10: The Second Continental Congress assembles in Philadelphia.

June 15: George Washington is named commander-in-chief of the Continental Army.

June 17: The Battle of Bunker Hill is fought—the British win but suffer heavy losses.

The Battle of Long Island, also called the Battle of Brooklyn, gave the British control of New York City.

1776

January 10: Thomas Paine's pamphlet *Common Sense* is published. It sets out clearly why the colonies should become independent from Great Britain.

July 4: The Declaration of Independence is ratified by the Continental Congress.

August 27: In the Battle of Long Island, the British drive back the Americans.

December 26: Washington launches a surprise attack in Trenton, New Jersey, and gains an important American victory. Eight days later, he again defeats the British at Princeton.

1780

September 25: As the war continues, Continental General Benedict Arnold's plans to surrender West Point to British forces are found out. He escapes and becomes a brigadier general in the British army.

1781

March 1: The Articles of Confederation are ratified by the Continental Congress. The document will later be replaced by the US Constitution.

1783

September 3: The Treaty of Paris ends the American Revolution.

CHAPTER 2

THE ROAD TO WAR

There were a number of reasons why colonists felt they were being treated unfairly. Deep in debt as a result of several wars, Britain was imposing new and increased taxes on its colonies. The Proclamation of 1763 also forbade colonists from settling in new territories, confining them to the East Coast.

Raising Money

The French and Indian War—part of a worldwide nine-year-long war between Great Britain and France—was fought over the colonies each held in North America. Although Great Britain won the war, it was left heavily in debt. As a result, it created new taxes on the colonies and raised existing taxes. The Sugar Act in 1764 placed a three-cent tax on sugar and raised the taxes on wine, coffee, and a type of dye called indigo. These products were important to colonial families, so the higher prices meant they had less

Because the British had fought the French and Indian War to protect the colonies, they believed colonists should share some of the costs.

money to spend on other things their families needed to survive. Meanwhile, those who sold the products worried that the taxes would ruin their businesses, and that they would not be able to support their families. Many in the colonies were not doing well financially at the time. People also worried about the future. Some colonists had hoped that the British victory in the French and Indian War would mean more land to settle with their families. However, to protect Native American territory, with the Proclamation of 1763, the British imposed—and enforced—new boundaries. Settlers who had bought land beyond these boundaries were forced to withdraw.

Protests Begin

In 1765, the Stamp Act was passed. It required colonists to pay a tax on printed materials, such as newspapers and legal documents. This further angered them, and people began to protest the new taxes. In 1766, both the Sugar Act and Stamp Act were repealed, but many colonists were becoming uneasy with the way that Great Britain was governing them.

Primary Source: What Does It Tell Us?

By 1770, tensions between colonists and British soldiers were high. On March 5, a small group of British soldiers fired into an angry crowd of colonists, killing five men. A few weeks later, Paul Revere published this engraving showing the event, called the Boston Massacre. Others who supported the British told a different version of the incident, which was more sympathetic to the soldiers. How do you think this engraving might have influenced colonists' feelings about the British?

TAXATION WITHOUT REPRESENTATION

The way that current US government is designed, elections are held in which people can vote on who will represent them in local, state, and federal government. Each state sends two representatives to the Senate and a certain number of representatives to the House of Representatives. Together, these two bodies make up the US Congress, which makes laws. Today, we often take it for granted that we have a say in how the government is run. However, this was not the case for colonists before the American Revolution.

"No Taxation Without Representation"

Though the British repealed the Sugar Act and the Stamp Act, they still believed they had a right to tax the colonies in any way they chose. They considered taxes to be no different from any other law. Many colonists, on the other hand, were beginning to wonder whether the British had the right to tax them without their consent.

With the passage of the Sugar Act, some colonists began to openly question why they should be taxed by the British Parliament when they were not represented in that parliament. This idea grew stronger with the passage of the Stamp Act and then the Townshend Acts, which included taxes on glass and paper. Colonists argued that, because they did not have a right to vote and send a representative to Parliament, the Parliament had no right to impose taxes on them.

Samuel Adams was active in Massachusetts politics. He argued that the Boston Tea Party was a principled protest to defend constitutional rights.

The Boston Tea Party

In 1773, the British passed the Tea Act. To help the British East India Company, which had an excess of tea stored in England, the act lowered the cost of tea sold to the colonies. This undercut local prices, and many colonists saw it as a way of forcing them to buy from the British company. On the night of December 16, a group of colonists called the Sons of Liberty dressed up as Native Americans. They then snuck aboard three East India Company ships in Boston Harbor, and dumped 342 crates of their tea into the water, destroying it.

Secondary Source: What Does It Tell Us?

This print was created in 1846, more than 70 years after the Boston Tea Party. Many of the men dumping the tea are dressed as members of the Mohawk tribe. At the time of the Revolution, Native Americans were often used as a symbol of America. Why do you think the men chose to disguise themselves as Mohawks?

THE DESTRUCTION OF TEA AT BOSTON HARBOR.

THE INTOLERABLE ACTS

The Boston Tea Party was an act of disobedience meant to show how far the colonists would go against the British. The event left the British angry and determined to punish those responsible. However, their retaliation would only serve to convince more colonists that independence might be the only answer.

Harsh New Laws

To punish the people of Massachusetts for the Boston Tea Party, the British Parliament passed a group of five laws in 1774. The British called these laws the Coercive Acts; the colonists named them the Intolerable Acts.

The first allowed the governor of a colony, who was appointed by the king, to move the trial of a royal official to another colony or even back to England if he believed a colonial jury would not be fair. Another act required nearly all appointments to governing positions in the Massachusetts Bay colony to be made by the governor, the king, or parliament. It also limited the number of town meetings Massachusetts colonists could hold.

The Boston Port Act closed Boston Harbor until the colonists paid for the tea ruined in the Boston Tea Party. The tea was worth about $1 million in today's money!

Primary Source: What Does It Tell Us?

This political cartoon was shared throughout the 13 colonies. The figure being held down represents the colonies, while the men pouring tea down the figure's throat represent England and the Intolerable Acts. What feelings might this cartoon and the Intolerable Acts have stirred in colonists who were already unsure about their loyalty to England?

The able Doctor, or America swallowing the Bitter Draught.

A third act allowed British troops to stay in the homes of colonists and other buildings. A fourth act closed Boston Harbor until the British East India Company had been repaid for the tea destroyed during the Boston Tea Party. A fifth act was favorable to Quebec, offering its French residents civil government and religious freedom. Although this last act was not directly related to the American colonies, many colonists considered it an insult.

The Acts Backfire

The Intolerable Acts were meant to stop the rebellious colonists. Instead, they made people even angrier, and led colonists to form the First Continental Congress to discuss what they should do.

CHAPTER 3

THE REVOLUTION BEGINS

Called in response to the Intolerable Acts, the First Continental Congress was a meeting of representatives from 12 of the 13 colonies. Its aim was to find a way to show the unity of the colonies to Great Britain, and to help resolve the problems between them.

Colonial Unity

The First Continental Congress met from September 5 to October 26, 1774, at Carpenter's Hall, in Philadelphia, Pennsylvania. It was attended by 56 delegates from 12 colonies. However, not all of the colonies had the same ideas of how to handle the British. Some wanted to convince Great Britain to repeal the Intolerable Acts and find a peaceful solution to the conflict. Some wanted to remain British colonies, but find a way to be represented in Parliament. Others wanted to cut ties with the British and become independent.

About 700 British soldiers met 77 members of the local soldiers in Lexington.

Paul Revere, seen here, rode to Lexington to warn Samuel Adams and John Hancock that the British planned to arrest them.

18

Lexington and Concord

The First Continental Congress had arranged for a further meeting to take place in May of 1775. Meanwhile, however, a rebel group in Massachusetts had begun to train a militia—a group of volunteer or citizen soldiers. Members of a militia were generally not well-trained fighters. They did not have uniforms and usually had to provide their own weapons. When the militia was needed in an emergency, the men had to leave their work, homes, and loved ones, not knowing when they might return.

Great Britain now considered Massachusetts to be in a state of rebellion. In April 1775, British troops were sent to destroy supplies being held by the militia in the town of Concord. On April 19, in Lexington, the British met the small local militia, who had been warned they were coming. Neither side expected a battle, but a gunshot went off, and the British began to fire. The militia retreated, and the British moved on to Concord. However, outside Concord more members of the militia gathered, and more shots were fired. This time, it was the British who retreated. The battles of Lexington and Concord are considered the beginning of the American Revolution.

Secondary Source: What Does It Tell Us?

These two verses are from "Concord Hymn," a poem commemorating the Battle of Concord, written by Ralph Waldo Emerson in 1837. If the British had won the war, what words might he have changed?

"By the rude bridge that arched the flood,
Their flag to April's breeze unfurled,
Here once the embattled farmers stood,
And fired the shot heard round the world.

Spirit, that made those heroes dare,
To die, and leave their children free,
Bid Time and Nature gently spare
The shaft we raise to them and thee."

THE SECOND CONTINENTAL CONGRESS

By the time the Second Continental Congress was due to meet, things had changed. The British and the colonists, often called the Patriots, were at war. The goals of the Second Continental Congress would be different from those of the first. However, it would face many of the same challenges.

Primary Source: What Does It Tell Us?

The Olive Branch Petition was written by Congress members led by John Dickinson, who wanted to emphasize their loyalty and make peace with Britain. It was sent to England in July 1775. However, a letter from John Adams, talking about going to war and capturing British officials, was discovered and sent to England at about the same time. As a result, King George declared the colonies in rebellion. Despite the pleading words in this extract from the petition, why do you think the king felt that revolution was inevitable?

"Could we represent in their full force the sentiments that agitate the minds of us your dutiful subjects, we are persuaded your Majesty would ascribe any seeming deviation from reverence in our language, and even in our conduct, not to any reprehensible intention, but to the impossibility of reconciling the usual appearances of respect with a just attention to our own preservation against those artful and cruel enemies who abuse your royal confidence and authority, for the purpose of effecting our destruction."

Reconciliation or Rebellion?

Many of the delegates from the First Continental Congress, such as John Adams and Roger Sherman, attended the Second Continental Congress, too. Benjamin Franklin, John Hancock, and Thomas Jefferson were also there. While many of the delegates still wanted to settle matters peacefully with the British and remain British colonies, a growing number believed independence was the only answer.

George Washington

The Second Continental Congress, which began meeting on May 10, 1775, in Philadelphia, quickly took charge of the war effort. On June 14, the Continental Army was created and George Washington appointed to be its commanding general. Washington, from Virginia, came from a wealthy family of tobacco farmers. He had been a senior officer during the French and Indian War and had seen firsthand the tactics, strengths, and weaknesses of the British army. This knowledge would be very valuable to the Patriots.

After the American Revolution, George Washington would go on to serve as the first president of the United States.

THE DECLARATION OF INDEPENDENCE

By the summer of 1776, the American Revolution had been going on for more than a year. The Continental Congress knew that they might need help in their fight against the British. However, they knew that no European country would make an alliance with the colonies while they were still under British control. They needed to declare themselves an independent country.

Drafting the Declaration

To create this declaration, the Congress appointed a group called the Committee of Five on June 11, 1776. The committee included Thomas Jefferson, John Adams, Roger Sherman, Robert R. Livingston, and Benjamin Franklin. The Committee of Five decided that Thomas Jefferson should write a draft of the declaration. Jefferson wrote a first draft, then brought it to the others to discuss and make changes. The committee wrote another draft, then presented it to the rest of the delegates on June 28. After more editing, the Congress voted to pass the Declaration of Independence on July 2. On July 4, the day now celebrated as Independence Day, the Declaration was finally adopted and printed for the general public.

On August 2, the Declaration of Independence was signed by 56 delegates. A few of the delegates, such as John Dickinson, refused to sign the document. Others signed, even though they had voted against its passage. Though they might not have agreed with the creation of a new independent country, they wanted to show a united front.

John Adams believed that July 2 should be celebrated, rather than July 4, since that was the day the Congress voted on independence.

Primary Source: What Does It Tell Us?

This pamphlet, called *Common Sense*, was written by Thomas Paine and published on January 10, 1776. The pamphlet encouraged colonists to support independence. It was very influential and changed many people's minds and loyalties toward Great Britain. Why was it so important for the revolution to have the support of ordinary colonists?

COMMON SENSE;

ADDRESSED TO THE *W. Hamilton*

INHABITANTS

OF

AMERICA,

On the following interesting

SUBJECTS.

I. Of the Origin and Design of Government in general, with concise Remarks on the English Constitution.

II. Of Monarchy and Hereditary Succession.

III. Thoughts on the present State of American Affairs.

IV. Of the present Ability of America, with some miscellaneous Reflections.

Man knows no Master save creating HEAVEN,
Or those whom choice and common good ordain.
THOMSON.

PHILADELPHIA;
Printed, and Sold, by R. BELL, in Third Street.
MDCCLXXVI.

The American Revolution lasted nearly eight years, from the first shot to the last. Over that time, there were many important battles between the Continental Army and the British Army. Some are considered important because of the high number of casualties. Others are remembered because they turned the tide of the war in one direction or the other. For the families who lived through the American Revolution, though, each casualty was devastating. These battles were not fought by professional soldiers, but by ordinary working colonists. The loss of a husband, father, son, or brother cost families dearly in both emotional and financial ways.

Beginning Battles

While the Battles of Lexington and Concord marked the start of the war, the next major turning point was the capture of Fort Ticonderoga in New York State, in May 1775. A small militia called the Green Mountain Boys raided Fort Ticonderoga and two other forts, capturing cannons and other military supplies. The artillery taken was brought to Massachusetts and used to force the British to withdraw from Boston.

Battle of Bunker Hill

The bloodiest battle of the war would occur just a month later. On June 17, colonial and British troops met at the Battle of Bunker Hill, near Boston. The British troops advanced on the colonial soldiers, who were holding Breed's Hill. During two assaults, the colonial forces fired on the lines of British soldiers, killing several officers and wounding hundreds. On their third advance, the British were able to take the hill, but many were killed, and more than 800 were wounded in the battle.

Secondary Source: What Does It Tell Us?

This painting, created nearly 70 years after the start of the American Revolution, shows colonials pulling down a statue of King George III in New York City. This event occurred on July 9, 1776, after the Declaration of Independence had been read aloud publicly. Notice that there are women and young children present. What do you think the mood would have been at this event?

At the Battle of Bunker Hill, colonial troops ran out of ammunition and fought by throwing rocks and swinging their muskets.

This famous painting shows Washington crossing the Delaware River before the Battle of Trenton.

Battle of Long Island

Also called the Battle of Brooklyn, this battle took place on August 27, 1776. It involved more troops than any other battle of the war. George Washington and his men were defeated trying to defend New York City and its harbor.

CHAPTER 4

WOMEN OF THE REVOLUTION

Martha Washington, wife of George Washington, spent winters with her husband at his army camps.

When wars are described, the focus is often on soldiers. Because women of the time had little voice in politics, it is also the important contributions of men, such as Thomas Jefferson and John Adams, that take center stage. Yet, in the American Revolution, women played an important role. Their support and sacrifices made the fighting possible.

The War Comes Home

Before the revolution, most colonists lived in rural areas outside of cities or large towns. Many either owned or worked on farms. While men were responsible for much of the farm labor, women took care of the household duties. They sewed, cleaned, washed clothes, and prepared food. Other tasks included gardening, milking cows, and preserving meats.

Homespun Support

As the revolution began, a woman's role in the household took on great significance. Although the governing bodies, made up of men, proposed boycotts of British goods, it fell to individual households–and especially women–to put these boycotts into action. During the revolution, women across the colonies stopped ordering clothes and fabrics from England. Many were active in the Homespun Movement, which encouraged women to weave and spin their own cloth instead of purchasing it from England. They also boycotted British tea and other goods. It became a point of pride to buy goods made in the colonies.

Financial Support

Women were also active in supporting the colonial troops. Many made blankets and clothing for the soldiers. They also raised money for the war effort through organizations such as the Ladies' Association.

Primary Source: What Does It Tell Us?

These are the words of Penelope Barker, a woman from North Carolina who organized the Edenton Tea Party. On October 25, 1775, 51 women signed a document stating their intent to boycott British tea and other goods. This was one of the first political actions by women in the colonies, and they were a major inspiration to many others. How do you think Barker's words might have rallied other women to the cause?

"Maybe it has only been men who have protested the king up to now. That only means we women have taken too long to let our voices be heard. We are signing our names to a document, not hiding ourselves behind costumes like the men in Boston did at their tea party. The British will know who we are."

27

WOMEN ON THE BATTLEFIELD

The colonial militias, and later the Continental Army, were not made up of professional soldiers, but of everyday colonists. Many of these men left their work and families behind when they went off to fight. Wives, mothers, sisters, and daughters had to look after homes, farms, and businesses. Instead of staying at home, however, some women chose to go off to war, too.

Camp Followers

A number of women chose to follow their husbands to the battlefield because they did not feel safe staying in their homes alone. This was especially true of women who lived in areas occupied by the British. Other women simply wanted to stay near their husbands. Women who accompanied men into army camps were called camp followers. They did not fight in battles, but they supported the men who did by cooking, washing and sewing clothes, and even acting as nurses. They helped with the everyday chores that allowed the camps to run smoothly. Some think there might have been as many as 20,000 women in army camps during the war.

Deborah Sampson successfully petitioned the government to give her a pension for her service during the war.

Molly Pitcher

It is not certain where the nickname "Molly Pitcher" came from, but the legend of Molly Pitcher is well known. It may have come from the real story of a camp follower named Mary Ludwig Hays. At the Battle of Monmouth, in June 1778, Mary Hays' husband was injured while firing a cannon. Mary Hays, who had been carrying water to the troops, took her husband's place and continued firing the cannon, even after she was almost hit by enemy fire.

Female Soldiers

Deborah Sampson did not follow a man into battle, but joined the Continental Army on her own. She dressed as a man and went by the name Robert Shurtlieff. She was wounded in the leg by two musket balls, but left the hospital before they could be removed, so that her identity would not be discovered.

This woman uses a spinning wheel in a reenactment of life in an army camp.

29

DIVIDED LOYALTIES

Before the time of the American Revolution, colonists considered themselves British, although they lived thousands of miles from England. For many, that loyalty to England did not end when the fighting began. The division between those who believed in independence and those who supported the British split families and turned neighbors and friends against each other.

Patriots and Loyalists

Colonists who believed in independence were called Patriots, while those who stayed loyal to England were called Loyalists. It is thought that about 20 percent of colonists remained loyal to England. Choosing whether to be a Patriot or a Loyalist was an important decision.

Families Torn Apart

Back then—as now—family members did not always agree with each other on political matters. Families were often torn apart, with some members calling themselves Loyalists and others calling themselves Patriots. It could be very difficult for women who disagreed with their husbands' positions.

Loyalist colonists did not want to go to war with the British, which often put them at odds with friends, neighbors, and family members.

Primary Source: What Does It Tell Us?

This image shows a Loyalist about to be tarred and feathered by a Patriot mob. Tarring and feathering a person meant covering him with a sticky tar and then covering him with feathers. Loyalist families during the revolution were often the target of threats, intimidation, and even violence. Do you think acts such as tarring and feathering were intended to humiliate them?

Women generally did not have a voice in politics. If a man was a Loyalist, it was assumed that his wife was as well, and then the entire family could be targeted.

During the Revolution, many women who strongly supported one side or the other began taking a public stance, even if it meant going against their husbands or other family members. While divorce had been very rare up to that time, the government began to allow Patriot women to divorce their Loyalist husbands.

Abigail Adams wrote hundreds of letters to her Patriot husband, John Adams, giving him advice on political matters.

Loyalist Women

The American Revolution could be a difficult time for women and families who supported the king. They often had their property seized by Patriot groups. If they wanted to leave the colonies, they were not allowed to take their possessions with them. Even so, many fled to Canada. Yet, if they did leave, any sons over the age of 12 could be compelled to stay and fight for the Patriots.

CHAPTER 5

CHILDREN AND FAMILIES

Children who lived in the colonies in the years before and during the American Revolution were greatly affected by the war. Many young men who would later fight for the Continental Army had been children when the Sugar Act and Stamp Act were passed. Children would see their fathers and older brothers leave to fight, unsure if they would ever come back.

During the Revolution, families taught their children about liberty and service so that these values would be passed on to future generations.

Life Before the War

Life for children in the years before the American Revolution was very different from what it is today. Young children often had many chores and responsibilities at home. If their families owned or worked on farms, they were expected to help with such things as milking cows and gathering eggs.

Not all children went to school in colonial times. Many attended small schools between the ages of 6 to 8. After that, generally, only the sons of wealthy families continued in school. Girls seldom stayed on at school; instead, they were expected to help their mothers with cooking, cleaning, and taking care of younger siblings.

Learning a Trade

When boys reached the age of about 14, or even younger, they often started an apprenticeship with older craftsmen or businessmen. In an apprenticeship, a boy's parents paid a blacksmith, printer, or other master craftsman to allow their son to study the trade for a certain number of years. The apprentice would live with the craftsman, away from his family, until he had mastered the trade.

Families in Danger

When the American Revolution began, many men and teenage boys left to fight. This meant that the women and children left behind had to take on new roles and responsibilities. The Continental and British armies would fight wherever they met up, which was often near peoples' homes. Many families had to flee to safety with very little warning. Others were forced to let soldiers live in their homes.

The legend of Nancy Hart says that she killed six British soldiers who came into her home and demanded that she should cook them dinner.

Young people who grew up in the years of the American Revolution often had strong opinions about the war. Many teenage boys and young men signed up to fight as soon as the war began. Younger children, both boys and girls, found ways to participate and support the war effort as well.

Boys on the Battlefield

Starting at the age of 16, boys could join the Continental and British armies. Some volunteered to join. Others were drafted, or required to join, for a certain period of time. It was not unusual for boys under the age of 16 to make it onto the battlefield, though. Boys as young as nine years old could join the troops as drummer boys. Drums were an important way for soldiers to communicate on the battlefield. Certain drum patterns stood for certain commands. Drummer boys also set the rhythm for marching and called soldiers to battle.

Together with young boys, men who were too old to fight also acted as drummers and musicians.

These words come from Joseph Plumb Martin, who joined the Connecticut state militia at the age of 15 and the Continental Army at 16, after being inspired by the battles of Lexington and Concord. Joseph Plumb Martin was from a wealthy family and was well educated. How do you think his description of battle contrasts with what his life was like before the war?

"The British took possession of a hill overlooking us. . . . During the night we remained in our trenches. . . . The water was nearly over my shoes by morning. Many of us took violent colds. . . . I had nothing to eat or drink, not even water. In the evening a messmate found me and brought me boiled hog's flesh and turnips."

These drummers are participating in a reenactment of the Battle of Yorktown.

Girls of the War

Boys were not the only ones eager to support their side. Sybil Ludington's father was a militia commander. When Sybil was 16 years old, she rode 40 miles (64 km) through dangerous terrain in the middle of the night to gather her father's troops and warn them of a British attack. Though they were not allowed to join the army, other girls throughout the colonies supported soldiers however they could. They cooked for the troops and sewed their uniforms. They also acted as nurses for the wounded.

The colonists were not the only people affected by the American Revolution. At the time of the war, hundreds of thousands of Native Americans lived in the lands that both the colonists and British were fighting for. The revolution would change their relationships with the colonists and with each other for generations.

Who to Support?

In the early stages of the American Revolution, most Native American tribes wanted to remain neutral—that is, they did not want to take sides in the conflict. Many soon realized, though, that an independent American country could be a bigger threat to their land and culture than the British colonies. While some Native American groups decided to side with the colonists, most sided with the British because the British had promised to protect their lands from white settlers. During the war, many Native Americans would be killed, either in battle, as retaliation by soldiers, or by starvation.

Primary Source: What Does It Tell Us?

On July 13, 1775, the Second Continental Congress approved this speech to the Six Nations. In it, they ask Native Americans to stay neutral. Why do you think the colonists did not want Native American groups involved in the war? Do you agree with the statement from the Congress that the war did not concern the Native Americans?

"We desire you will hear and receive what we have now told you, and that you will open a good ear and listen to what we are now going to say. This is a family quarrel between us and Old England. You Indians are not concerned in it. We don't wish you to take up the hatchet against the king's troops. We desire you to remain at home, and not join on either side, but keep the hatchet buried deep."

Changing Roles

When the war was over, Native Americans did not get the protections they had hoped for. Instead, the United States continued to expand westward and many tribes were forced off their land. The policies of the newly created United States also forced Native American groups to stop hunting and survive instead on agriculture, or growing crops. Agriculture had traditionally been the responsibility of women in the tribes, so this was a major shift in roles.

Joseph Louis Cook sided with the colonists and became the highest-ranking Native American in the Continental Army.

CHAPTER 6

A NEW NATION

After nearly eight years of fighting and many more of political unrest, the American Revolution ended in 1783. The British and the colonists signed a peace treaty and British troops left the former colonies. The new geographic boundaries of the country that would become the United States were set. For families who had once considered themselves British citizens, it was now time to become Americans.

The Siege of Yorktown

The last major battle was in September and October 1781. The British army, led by General Charles Cornwallis, had retreated to Yorktown, Virginia. The French, allies of the colonists, sent ships to Virginia to stop the British from leaving Yorktown. Meanwhile, George Washington marched his troops south toward Yorktown. The British were surrounded and outnumbered by the 18,000 Continental and French troops. On October 19, Cornwallis surrendered to Washington, and about 7,000 British troops were captured.

Shown here is Cornwallis's surrender. Many of the British soldiers at Yorktown were suffering from malaria and unable to fight.

Secondary Source: What Does It Tell Us?

The painting, by Benjamin West, shows the signing of a preliminary peace agreement between the Americans and the British. The Americans, including Benjamin Franklin and John Adams, are shown on the left side. However, the British representatives refused to pose for the painting and it was never finished. What might this tell you about how some in Great Britain felt about the peace agreement?

During the peace negotiations, the province of Quebec, in what is now eastern Canada, almost became part of the United States.

Peace Treaty

The British defeat at Yorktown convinced many in England that they should stop fighting. In February 1782, the British Parliament voted to end the war. In April, negotiations began between the British and the Americans. Benjamin Franklin, John Jay, Henry Laurens, and John Adams represented the Americans in the peace talks. After nearly a year and a half, on September 3, 1783, the Treaty of Paris was signed. The United States now included the land stretching down to Florida in the south, what is now Canada to the north, and the Mississippi River to the west.

CREATING A NEW COUNTRY

During the American Revolution, the Continental Congress had written a framework for a new government called the Articles of Confederation. It was an agreement between the 13 states. It dealt with issues such as taxes that would be paid, and how each state would vote to pass laws that applied to the entire country. It also stated that all 13 states had to agree before the Articles of Confederation could be amended, or changed.

A Broken Framework

Once the United States had won the Revolution and began to fully function as a new country, the Articles of Confederation were found to have many problems. Congress did not have the structure or powers to raise money by collecting taxes, or to force states to follow laws that were created.

In 1787, it was decided that a new framework was needed. A convention was called to create it. After months of debate and compromises, the US Constitution was written and approved by the convention delegates. It then went to the states for ratification. Nine states needed to ratify it before the Constitution was accepted. On June 21, 1788, the ninth state ratified it, and the Constitution took effect in 1789. By 1790, the thirteenth and last state, Rhode Island, ratified the document.

The Constitution was originally composed of a preamble (introductory statement) and seven articles.

The Constitution was signed by the delegates on September 17, 1787.

The framework of government created by the Constitution is still used. Here, the president addresses a joint session of Congress.

Checks and Balances

The US Constitution is short compared to the constitutions of many other countries, but it lays the framework for how the US government still works today. In it, the federal, or central, government is divided into three branches—executive, legislative, and judicial. The legislative branch includes the Congress and makes the laws. The executive branch includes the president and enforces the laws. The judicial branch, which includes the Supreme Court, interprets the laws. By dividing the government into three branches, the Constitution ensures that no one person or group becomes too powerful.

LEGACY OF THE REVOLUTION

The men who would become the first five presidents of the United States had all played a major part in the Revolution. The sixth, John Quincy Adams, was a child during the war, and watched the Battle of Bunker Hill from the top of a hill when he was just seven years old! The men, women, and children who lived through the American Revolution would go on to shape the government that we live with today.

Making Changes

Though the Constitution was eventually ratified by all 13 states, not everyone believed that it was perfect. Many were concerned that it did not protect certain freedoms. As a solution, 10 amendments were added in 1791. These first 10 amendments are called the Bill of Rights. Many of the freedoms and protections that we now take for granted are listed in the Bill of Rights. These include the freedom of religion and the right to a trial by jury. Over time, a total of 27 amendments have been made to the Constitution. These amendments have established important changes, such as abolishing slavery and giving women the right to vote.

The March on Washington in 1963 is an important example of people using their right to free speech to promote social change.

Before the Bill of Rights guaranteed freedom of speech, people could be arrested, punished, or even killed for disagreeing with the government.

The United States Today

In the 1970s, the United States commemorated the bicentennial, or 200th, anniversary of the events leading up to its creation. Through speeches, museum exhibits, television specials, and fireworks, Americans celebrated their country and its road to independence.

Primary Source: What Does It Tell Us?

One of the freedoms listed in the Bill of Rights is the freedom of speech, which allows people to speak out against the government without the fear of being arrested. The people who demanded this freedom had lived through the Revolution, and the divisions and violence between those who supported the British and those who chose independence. Why would this right have been seen as especially important?

LIFE AFTER THE REVOLUTION

The American Revolution is the war that created the country America is today. It shaped US laws, the way citizens vote in elections and choose representatives in government, and the freedoms that the United States protects. We live with its legacy and effects every day.

Support and Sacrifice

Between 25,000 and 50,000 colonial soldiers were killed during the American Revolution. At least 8,000, though possibly many more, died on the battlefield. Another 17,000 were killed by disease or starvation. The casualties on the British side were about the same, with most deaths due to disease.

As with so many wars, the American Revolution was much more than a list of battles lost or won. It was an uneven struggle for independence, only achieved through the courage and sacrifices of those who fought in the Continental Army and the militias, and the women and children who supported them and took on new roles and responsibilities. Most suffered great personal losses as each side fought for the cause they believed in. All who lived through the American Revolution had to cope with the changes and adjustments of fighting against a country they had once called their own.

The United States has erected many memorials to the heroes of the American Revolution.

44

This memorial, installed in 1860, depicts George Washington during the Battle of Princeton.

John Paul Jones—considered the father of the US navy—is honored with this memorial in Washington, D.C.

An Enduring Legacy

For all of the suffering and hardship that the war brought colonial families, much was also gained. Together, the citizens of the newly formed United States worked to build a new country and unique system of government. For more than 200 years, the framework and government structure they created has both endured and influenced the governments of other countries. Their contributions are felt every day, around the world and here at home.

GLOSSARY

alliance group joining forces to work together

amendment addition or a change to a document, law, or set of laws, such as the Constitution

apprenticeship period during which a young person learns practical skills from someone more experienced in a skill, trade, or business

artillery cannons, large guns, or other weapons for firing over long distances

boycotts joining with others in refusing to buy from or deal with a person, nation, or business

casualties people who are injured or killed in an accident or war

charter official document that sets outs rights and establishes principles and rules

colonies areas of land controlled and often occupied by another—usually distant—country

committee group of people directed to oversee or consider a matter

delegates representatives elected to attend a political gathering

draft nonfinal version of a document

Loyalists people who were faithful to the British Crown during the American Revolution

malnutrition unhealthy condition caused by not having enough of the right types of food

militia group of volunteer or citizen soldiers, organized to assemble in emergencies

natural resources useful supplies of things that occur in nature, such as wood or animal furs

Parliament in England, the group of politicians who establish the country's laws

Patriots American colonists who believed in independence—separating from British rule

proprietary colonies privately owned colonies or settlements

ratified officially approved

repealed withdrew and did away with (a law)

royal colonies colonies controlled by a British governor, appointed by the king

Sons of Liberty secretive group of American colonists who organized widespread and sometimes violent protests against the British government's taxes and unfair treatment

taxes money added to the price of something or paid directly to fund government spending

treaty official, signed agreement between two or more groups or countries

US Constitution document adopted in 1788 that explains the different parts of the US government and how each part works

FOR MORE INFORMATION

Books

Bearce, Stephanie. *The American Revolution: Spies, Secret Missions, and Hidden Facts From the American Revolution* (Top Secret Files). Austin, TX: Prufrock Press, 2014.

Burgan, Michael. *The Split History of the American Revolution* (Perspectives Flip Books). North Mankato, MN: Compass Point Books, 2013.

Forest, Christopher. *The Biggest Battles of the Revolutionary War.* Mankato, MN: Capstone Press, 2013.

Huey, Lois Miner. *Voices of the American Revolution: Stories From the Battlefields.* (Voices of War). Mankato, MN: Capstone Press, 2011.

Websites

Find out more about the American Revolution at:
www.pbs.org/ktca/liberty/index.html

Learn about events, battle sites, leading Revolutionary figures, and much more at:
http://www.nps.gov/revwar/about_the_revolution/overview.html

Discover more about the constitution of the United States at:
http://bensguide.gpo.gov/3-5/documents/constitution

Publisher's note to educators and parents: Our editors have carefully reviewed these websites to ensure that they are suitable for students. Many websites change frequently, however, and we cannot guarantee that a site's future contents will continue to meet our high standards of quality and educational value. Be advised that students should be closely supervised whenever they access the Internet.

INDEX